YOUNG READERS' NATURE LIBRARY

THE EARTH

Keith Lye

MITCHELL · BEAZLEY
MILLBROOK

Series Editor: Julia Gorton
Editors: Heather Amery and Anita Ganeri
Designers: Pauline Bayne and Ann Burnham
Art Editor: Rowena Alsey
Picture Research: Lakshmi Hughes and Elizabeth Weiley
Typesetter: Kerri Hinchon
Production: Sarah Schuman

Cover illustration by David Nockels/Garden Studio
Additional illustrations by Graham Humphreys,
Andrew Farmer, Pavel Kostal, Chris Forsey, Peter Sarson, Colin Rose,
Susan Robertson, Graham Rosewarne, Tony Roberts, Barnaby Gorton

Published in 1991 by
Hamlyn Children's Books,
part of Reed International Books Ltd.,
Michelin House, 81 Fulham Road,
London SW3 6RB

Published in the United States by
The Millbrook Press, 2 Old New Milford Road,
Brookfield, Connecticut

Cataloging-in-Publication Data

Lye, Keith
The earth/by Keith Lye

64p.; col. ill.; maps: (Young Readers' Nature Library)
Includes index.

Summary: A comprehensive illustrated survey of the
Earth's structure, weather, metals and minerals, environments,
and life on land and in the oceans.
The future of our planet is discussed.

ISBN 1-56294-025-2

1. Earth - Crust. 2. Earth - Internal Structure. 3. Earth sciences.
4. Endangered species. I. Title. II. Series.

1991

551.1 LYE

Typeset in Bembo
Linotronic Output by Tradespools Ltd, Frome, Somerset
Origination by Mandarin Offset, Hong Kong
Produced by Mandarin Offset, Hong Kong

Contents

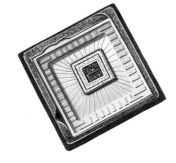
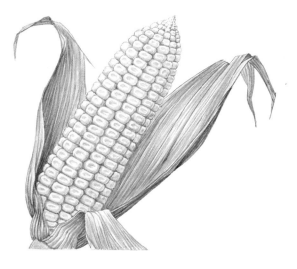

4   All About the Earth
6   The Story of the Earth
8   The Earth in Space
10 Inside the Earth
12 The Oceans
14 The Changing Land
16 Earthquakes
18 Volcanoes
20 Mountains
22 Under the Ground
24 Rivers and Glaciers
26 Weather and Climate
28 The Atmosphere
30 Rain, Snow, and Hail
32 The Weather
34 Climates
36 The Dry Places
38 Mild Climates
40 Cold Places
42 The Planet and Its People
44 Where People Live
46 Towns and Cities
48 What People Eat
50 The World's Farmers
52 The Earth's Resources
54 Minerals, Metals, and Energy
56 Using the Earth's Resources
58 Damaging the Earth
60 The Earth's Future
62 Glossary
63 Index

All About the Earth

Our Earth is a huge ball made of rocks and metals. It travels around the sun, like a giant spacecraft, and has all the things that we, the passengers, need on our journey.

A being from outer space, looking down on the Earth, would probably call it "Water" or "Ocean." This is because water covers more than seven tenths of the Earth's surface. From space, the oceans look blue.

The Continents

Land covers less than three tenths of the Earth and is divided into seven continents. The largest continent is Asia, followed by Africa, North America, South America, Antarctica, Europe, and Australia.

The Crust

The rocky continents and the rocks under the oceans form a thin, hard layer, called the crust. Beneath the crust are hot rocks and metal. No one has ever drilled through the crust to get samples of the rocks under it.

Blanket of Air

The Earth is surrounded by air. Air is a mixture of gases, including oxygen, which we need to breathe, and carbon dioxide, which plants use to make oxygen. The air around the Earth is called the atmosphere.

The Story of the Earth

The Earth is about 4.6 billion years old. For millions of years, its surface was covered by hot, liquid rock. Gases and steam escaped from the fiery rocks to form the Earth's first atmosphere.

After many millions of years, the Earth's surface started to cool and a thin crust began to form. This crust was often broken up and remelted. As it took shape, water filled the hollows to form the first lakes and seas.

The Earth Forms

The Earth, along with the other planets, probably formed from a vast cloud of gas and dust spinning around the sun. This material slowly collected into separate masses, which became the nine planets and their moons. Gradually, over many millions of years, the Earth changed from a large, hot ball of gas and dust to a smaller, cooler, rocky planet.

The first amphibians (animals that live partly on land and partly in water) lived in the Devonian period.

Reptiles appeared in the Carboniferous period, when much of the Earth was covered in dense vegetation.

Devonian 395–350 mya

Silurian 425–395 mya

Ordovician 500–425 mya

Fishes, the first animals with backbones, lived in the Ordovician period.

Carboniferous 350–290 mya

Permian 290–235 mya

The Fossil Record

Fossils show that many strange animals and plants once lived on Earth. They form in several ways. Whole insects are sometimes found preserved in amber, hardened resin from ancient trees (**A**).

Fossils of plant leaves (**B**), often found in coal, are called carbon smears. The leaf patterns are preserved as a thin film of carbon.

Many fossils in rock form when part of an animal or plant is buried in mud, which is later pressed into hard rock. The parts of the living thing then dissolve away, leaving a hole or mold. Minerals fill the mold to form a "cast." This shows the shape of a creature's shell, such as an ammonite (**C**).

Many different kinds of insects appeared in the Permian period.

A

B

C

Earth History Facts

The oldest known rocks are about 3.9 billion years old. Crystals found in a rock in Australia are 4.2 billion years old.

The oldest known fossils, about 3.5 billion years old, are traces of simple organisms called bacteria.

Early plants, growing in the seas 1.9 billion years ago, gradually produced enough oxygen to make the air breathable.

mya = million years ago

Precambrian 4,600–570 mya

Cambrian 570–500 mya

Trilobites - ancient creatures with shells, related to today's crabs and woodlice - appeared in the Cambrian period.

Life Emerges

The Earth seems to be the only planet in our solar system that supports life. Life on Earth probably began with tiny, simple creatures called bacteria. Over many millions of years, living things developed, or evolved, to produce the enormous variety of plants and animals that exist today.

An important stage in the Earth's history began about 570 million years ago when animals with hard parts evolved. The remains of some of these ancient living things are well preserved in rocks as fossils. The study of rocks and their fossils gives scientists important clues to the Earth's past.

Flying reptiles, alive at the time of the dinosaurs, may be the ancestors of modern birds.

Triassic 235–190 mya

Jurassic 190–130 mya

The dinosaurs reigned during the Jurassic period.

After the dinosaurs had died out at the end of the Cretaceous period, more and more mammals began to appear.

Cretaceous 130–65 mya

Tertiary 65–1.8 mya

"Apelike people" first appeared in the late Quaternary period.

Quaternary 1.8 mya until now

7

The Earth in Space

Planet Earth may seem very large to us, but it is really only a tiny speck in the universe. It is one of nine planets that hurtle around a star – our sun – in the solar system. The sun is just one of almost countless stars in the Milky Way Galaxy. The Milky Way is only one of over 400 million galaxies in the universe.

The Earth is always moving. It spins like a top all the time, taking 24 hours to make one complete turn. It also moves around the sun, taking one year to complete each journey or orbit. Finally, the Earth takes part in the 200-million-year journey of the solar system around the Milky Way Galaxy.

The Planets

The Earth is the third planet from the sun. Like Mercury, Venus, and Mars, the Earth is a small planet, made up mostly of rock and metal. Jupiter, Saturn, Uranus, and Neptune are giant planets, made mainly of gas. Scientists know little about Pluto, the most distant planet.

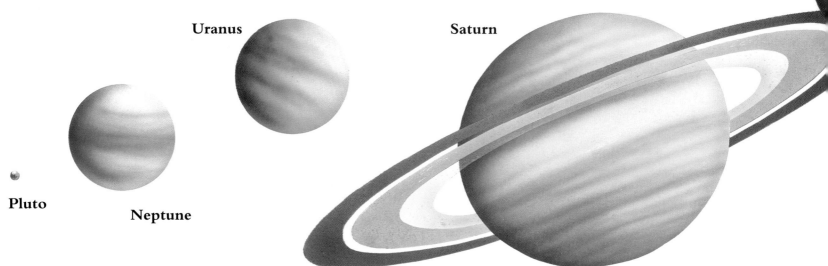

Uranus

Saturn

Pluto

Neptune

Day and Night

The Earth spins on its axis, making one complete turn in 24 hours. The axis is an imaginary line from the North Pole to the South Pole. The Equator is an imaginary line around the Earth, halfway between the North and South Poles.

Day and night are caused by the spin of the Earth. The side of the Earth facing the sun has daylight. The side away from the sun is dark and it is night.

Earth Facts

The Earth is not perfectly round but is slightly flattened at the Poles and bulges a little just south of the Equator. The distance around the Equator is 24,902 mi (40,075 km) while the distance around the Poles is 42 mi (68 km) shorter.

The Earth takes 365 days, 5 hours and 40 minutes to travel once in its orbit around the sun. The distance between the Earth and the sun is about 93 million mi (150 million km).

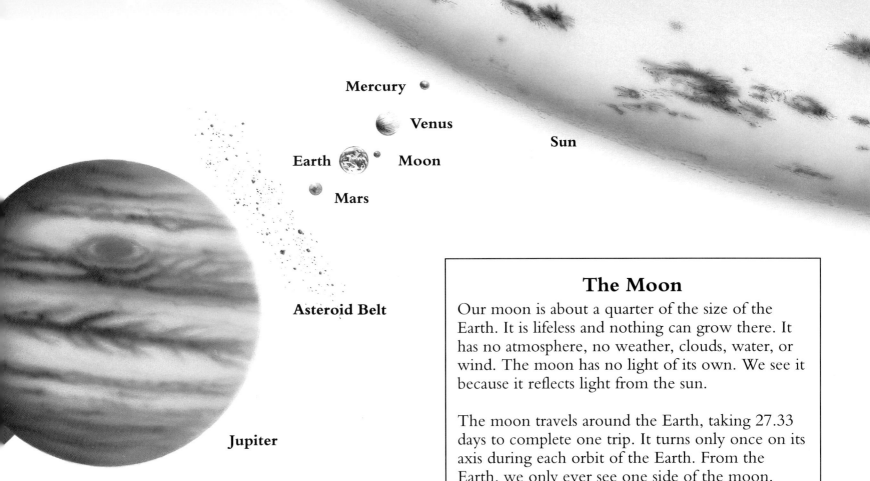

Mercury

Venus

Earth Moon

Mars

Sun

Asteroid Belt

Jupiter

The Moon

Our moon is about a quarter of the size of the Earth. It is lifeless and nothing can grow there. It has no atmosphere, no weather, clouds, water, or wind. The moon has no light of its own. We see it because it reflects light from the sun.

The moon travels around the Earth, taking 27.33 days to complete one trip. It turns only once on its axis during each orbit of the Earth. From the Earth, we only ever see one side of the moon.

Moon

The Sun

The sun is a giant star that we see during the day. It is a very hot ball of mostly hydrogen gas that burns with nuclear reactions at its center.

Without the sun's heat and light, there would be no life on Earth. The sun will eventually burn up all its gases and die, but not for 5 billion years.

Moon Rock

Astronauts who landed on the moon collected and brought back many samples of rock.

The oldest moon rocks were formed at about the same time as the Earth, about 4.6 billion years ago.

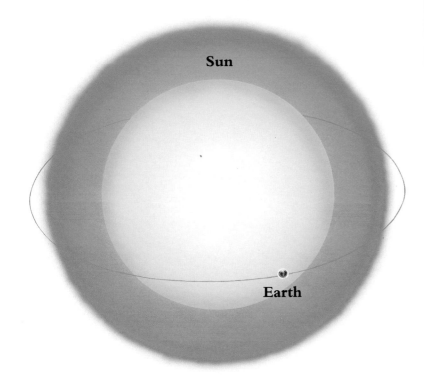

Sun

Earth

Inside the Earth

The Earth is a little like an onion. If you could cut the Earth in half, you would see that it is made up of layers. On the outside is the thin crust. Under the crust are three main layers, called the mantle, the outer core, and the inner core.

The Earth's crust and the top part of the mantle are made of solid rock. This layer of rock is split into several large pieces called plates. The plates are shifted around by movements in a layer of partly molten, or liquid, rock near the top of the mantle.

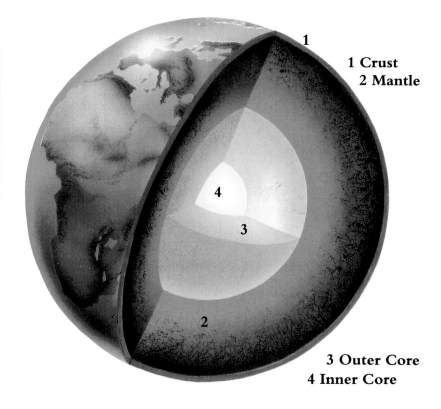

1 Crust
2 Mantle

3 Outer Core
4 Inner Core

Moving Continents

The Earth's surface is cracked into seven giant plates and several smaller ones. These plates consist of the crust and the top part of the mantle that rests on the partly molten rock. The molten rock moves very slowly, shifting the plates and carrying the continents around the world, like a giant jigsaw puzzle.

Some plates move apart along undersea mountain ranges called ocean ridges. As they separate, molten rock rises and forms new rock in the gaps. In other places, plates bump against each other and one plate is pushed underneath the other. The plate that is pushed downward into the mantle is melted and destroyed.

Under the sea, where two plates are moving apart, molten rock, or magma, wells up to fill the gap and cools on the sea floor.

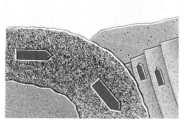

Where two plates meet, one may slide over the other. The edge of the lower one is pushed down and melted in the mantle.

Down into the Earth

The Earth's crust is about 25 mi (40 km) thick on the continents and only about 3 mi (5 km) thick under the oceans. Under the crust is the mantle, which is about 1,800 mi (2,900 km) thick.

Part of the upper mantle, under the solid outer layers, is partly molten rock that moves about very slowly, like thick molasses. This layer lies between 47 and 155 mi (75 and 250 km) below the surface.

The hot core is about 4,312 mi (6,940 km) across and is mainly iron. The outer core is liquid and the inner core is solid.

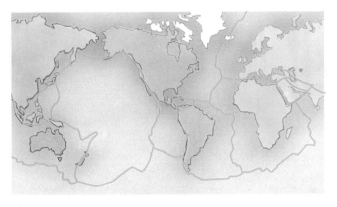

The Earth's Plates

This map shows the Earth's plates. Earthquakes and volcanic eruptions are common near the edges of the plates. The moving plates change the positions of the continents and slowly alter the world map.

Plate Facts

The plates under the Atlantic Ocean are moving apart by about half an inch (1 to 2 cm) a year. The fastest plate movement – 3 to 4 in (8 to 10 cm) a year – is in the southeastern Pacific Ocean.

Although plate movements are very slow, they have been going on for hundreds of millions of years. At the rate of 0.8 in (2 cm) a year, a plate will move 1,200 mi (2,000 km) in 100 million years.

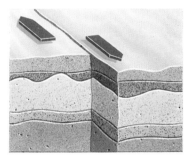

Some plates slide past each other along a huge fault, or crack, in the ground. As they move, the land shakes and there are giant earthquakes.

In some places where two plates meet and continents collide, the crust piles up to form mountain ranges.

The Oceans

Until recently, no one had explored or mapped the ocean floor, although salt water covers more than seven tenths of the Earth's surface. We now know that there are high mountains, deep trenches, and volcanoes hidden from sight under the waves.

Under the Water

Around most continents are shallow seas. They cover gently sloping coasts, called continental shelves. The oceans really begin at the steep continental slopes that lead down to the ocean deeps. On the ocean floor are huge plains as well as volcanic mountains, some of which rise above the water as islands. Great ocean ridges run through the oceans. The deepest parts of the oceans are the trenches, where one plate of the Earth's crust is being pushed beneath another.

The Tides

Tides are rises and falls in sea level that occur twice every 24 hours and 50 minutes. They are caused mainly by the moon. When the moon is overhead, its gravity pulls the water toward it, making the seas bulge.

The tides move around the oceans as the Earth spins. High tides occur when the Earth, moon, and sun are in line and the sun's pull is added to the moon's. Lower tides occur when the moon, Earth, and sun form a right angle and the moon's pull is partly balanced by the sun.

On the Move

Ocean water is always moving. It splashes on the shore as breaking waves. Waves are heaped up by wind blowing across open water. Light winds cause ripples but strong winds make waves 40 ft (12 m) high or more. Waves can wear away coasts and shorelines, batter rocks and cliffs, and smash buildings close to the shore.

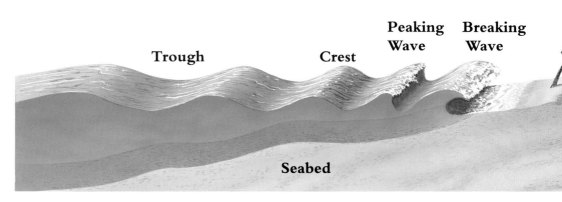

Trough   **Crest**   **Peaking Wave**   **Breaking Wave**

Seabed

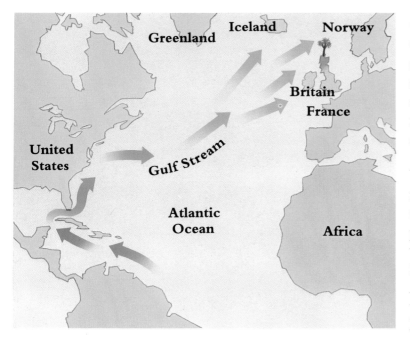

Greenland   Iceland   Norway   Britain   France   Gulf Stream   United States   Atlantic Ocean   Africa

Ocean Currents

Currents move water about and it is never quite still, even in the deepest ocean. Surface currents, mainly caused by winds, affect only about the top 1,150 ft (350 m) of water. Warm surface currents flow from the Equator toward the Poles, while deep cold polar ones move the other way. The warm Gulf Stream, flowing across the Atlantic, brings mild winters to northern Europe and Iceland.

Ocean Facts

The Pacific, the biggest ocean, is larger than all of the Earth's land area added together. It covers an area of about 64,186,000 sq mi (166,241,000 sq km).

The deepest place in the sea is in the Marianas Trench in the Pacific. The water there is 36,198 ft (11,033 m) deep.

The Changing Land

The Earth's surface is always changing very slowly. Millions of years ago, the map of the world looked very different from the one we know today.

Movements of the plates of the Earth's crust have shifted the continents and altered the shape of the oceans. Over millions of years, they have pushed up great mountain ranges and created deep valleys. Some coasts have heaved up to form cliffs while others have sunk beneath the sea.

The landscapes are also changing. Natural forces, such as rivers and glaciers, gradually wear away the land, hollowing out valleys and gorges. Water washes away rocks and soil and carves out underground caves. Wind, carrying dust, erodes rocks and heaps up great sand dunes.

Earthquakes and volcanic eruptions can cause sudden change. Erupting volcanoes may form new mountains and even new islands.

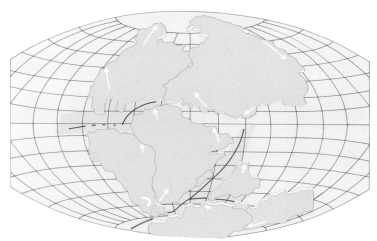

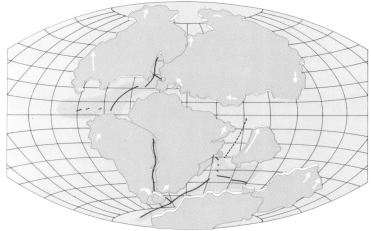

180 million
years ago

135 million
years ago

Drifting Continents

About 275 million years ago, the world map looked very different. All the land was joined together in one supercontinent which scientists call Pangaea. About 180 million years ago, Pangaea began to break up into pieces, pulled apart by the moving plates of the crust.

By 135 million years ago, North America was moving away from Europe. A new ocean, the North Atlantic, was growing wider. Australia and Antarctica began to move away from Africa. A plate bearing India was moving north toward Asia, and a gap had opened up between Africa and South America.

14

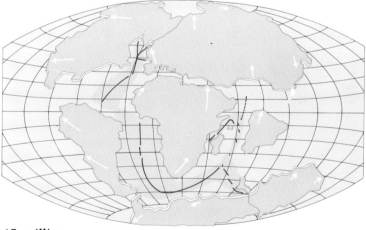

**65 million
years ago**

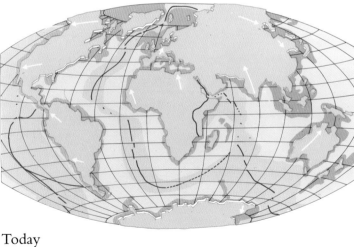

Today

About 65 million years ago, the continents began to look more as they do today. South America had drifted away from Africa, but Australia and Antarctica were still joined together. Greenland had still to separate from Europe. North America had begun to break away from Eurasia, as the rift in the North Atlantic grew.

Today's map shows that the Atlantic is now a wide ocean, stretching from the Arctic in the north to the Antarctic in the south. North and South America have joined up and India has collided with Asia, pushing up the Himalayas. All the continents that once made up Pangaea are now separated by wide oceans.

Earthquakes

Earthquakes happen very suddenly and without any warning. When the ground shakes, tall buildings rock and sway, and sometimes collapse, killing many people. Fires start when gas pipes are broken and electric cables snap. Great cracks may open up in the ground, destroying roads and railway lines. In the mountains, earthquakes may cause landslides and avalanches.

Earthquakes can occur anywhere on land, or on the ocean floor, when rocks move along faults in the Earth's crust. The worst earthquakes take place in areas near the edges of continental plates.

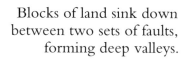

Blocks of land sink down between two sets of faults, forming deep valleys.

A block of land may move sideways along a deep fault.

Great Faults

Faults are huge cracks in rocks on the Earth's surface, along which the rocks have moved. They are often formed when the plates are pulled apart, stretching the rocks near the plate's edge. They also form when the plates are pushed against each other, bending the rocks.

Some faults can be seen quite clearly on the Earth's surface. Rocks may move sideways along these faults. In 1906, an earthquake struck the city of San Francisco, California. During this earthquake, the rocks along the huge San Andreas Fault moved sideways by up to 20 ft (6 m).

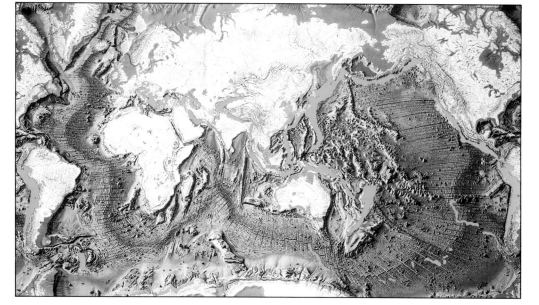

Earthquake Areas

Danger Zones

This map gives an idea of what the Earth would look like if it had no oceans. It shows the seabeds, with all their mountains, long, broken fault lines and deep trenches.

The long fault lines and the trenches show the edges of some of the moving plates of the Earth's crust. The plate edges are where earthquakes most often occur.

Instruments detect an average of 500,000 earthquakes per year. Only about 1 in 5 are strong enough for people to notice them, and only about 1 in 500 cause any damage.

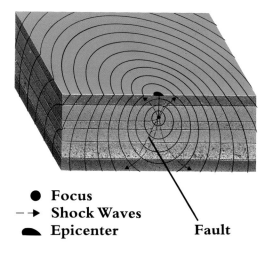

● **Focus**
– ➤ **Shock Waves**
🖤 **Epicenter**　　　　**Fault**

Earthquake Centers

The point inside the Earth where rocks move, causing an earthquake, is called the focus. The focus of many earthquakes is a long way down below the surface. Stress builds up at the focus as rocks are pushed by plate movement.

When the rocks finally break, shock waves move out from the focus in all directions. The rocks crack and shudder apart along the fault line and the ground shakes as shock waves reach the surface.

Earthquakes with a deep focus do less damage than those with a shallow one. The focus of a shallow earthquake is within about 40 mi (60 km) of the surface. Scientists use the term epicenter for the point on the Earth's surface that is directly above the focus.

Enormous Waves

Many earthquakes happen far out under the oceans where they do little harm. Earthquakes that take place on the seabed close to land can cause great damage.

These earthquakes may cause giant waves, called tsunamis. The waves can be more than 30 ft (10 m) high and travel at great speeds. Tsunami in the Pacific roar along as fast as a jet airplane. The waves may be over 60 mi (100 km) long.

When a tsunami reaches shallow water around a coast, it grows taller and crashes on the shore. It may smash harbors and buildings, drown many people, and carry ships far inland.

Earthquake Facts

An earthquake in east central China in 1556 killed more than 800,000 people.

An earthquake near Tokyo, Japan, in 1923 caused damage to property that was valued at millions of dollars. Today the same damage would cost many billions.

In Alaska in 1964, a very strong earthquake shook the ground for about 7 minutes. Some areas of land were raised or lowered by up to 56 ft (17 m) and huge tsunami swept ships inland.

Volcanoes

When volcanoes erupt, they can cause enormous damage, destroying whole towns, and killing hundreds, even thousands, of people. Volcanoes sometimes hurl clouds of ash into the air, burying nearby cities. Hot gases or streams of liquid rock may set fire to trees and vegetation, and burn forests, crops, and large areas of countryside.

Volcanic eruptions show that there are enormous forces inside the Earth. The word volcano means an opening in the ground, from which molten lava (hot, liquid rock), gases, and steam reach the surface. It also means a mountain made of hardened lava. But soils formed from hardened lava are very rich in minerals and produce good crops.

Underground Forces

Underneath volcanoes are large amounts of molten rock, called magma. The magma rises to the surface under pressure. At the surface, the magma is called lava. Some volcanoes spill out long streams of liquid lava. In others, the magma is broken into lumps or fine ash, and hurled into the air.

Many volcanoes are made of layers of lava and layers of ash. These volcanoes are usually cone-shaped. Volcanoes that erupt liquid lava are often shaped like upturned saucers.

Magma forms lava and ash during an eruption.

Lava and gases come out of cracks on the side of a volcano.

Each eruption adds a new layer, building up the cone of the volcano.

The lava from fissure eruptions is very fluid indeed. This lava may "flood" a large area, but it does not form volcanoes.

Water seeps down, is heated by the magma, and bubbles up as hot springs and geysers.

Most volcanoes are near the edges of the continental plates. Many grow from the ocean floor, along ocean ridges where plates are moving apart. Others are near ocean trenches where one plate is being pushed under another and melted.

A few volcanoes, such as those in Hawaii in the Pacific Ocean, lie far away from the plate edges. Here, lava from the volcanoes built up the islands. Scientists think that they are formed above sources of heat, or "hot spots," in the Earth's mantle.

Most active volcanoes only erupt now and then, sometimes not for hundreds of years. In between eruptions, scientists call them dormant, or sleeping. Old volcanoes that will never erupt again are said to be extinct, or dead.

Types of Volcanoes

The lava from the volcanoes on the Hawaiian Islands is quite runny and forms low mountains.

This type of eruption sends a tall column of ash and smoke high into the air, forming a thick cloud.

When the chimney of a volcano is blocked, it may erupt with a massive explosion.

This type of volcano erupts violently, throwing out red-hot lumps of solid lava.

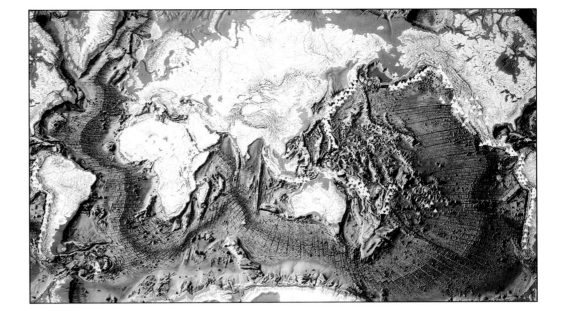

Volcano Areas

Volcano Facts

There are more than 1,300 active volcanoes in the world, many of which rise from the ocean floor. Only about 20 to 30 of these erupt in any one year.

The greatest known eruption was on the Greek island of Santorini in 1628 B.C.

Huge Eruption

In May 1980, Mount St. Helens, a volcano in the state of Washington, erupted. An earthquake shattered the north side, starting an avalanche of ice, rock, and mud. Hot gases and ash poured down the mountain, sweeping away the trees. A huge cloud of gas and ash shot 12 mi (20 km) into the air. The eruption blasted 1,312 ft (400 m) off the top of the volcano.

Mountains

The mountains of the world have been pushed up from the surface of the Earth in different ways. Some mountains are volcanoes. Some are dome mountains, pushed up by rising magma that does not reach the surface. Some mountains grew when rocks were squeezed up into great folds, while others are blocks of land pushed by the movements of the Earth's plates.

The world's greatest mountain ranges were formed by sideways pressure, caused when plates pushed against each other. The rocks that make up some of the world's highest peaks were formed on the ocean floor. Over thousands of years, these rocks were squeezed up into great folds.

Avalanche

Landslide

Growing Mountains

India and Asia were once separated by sea. About 50 million years ago, the slowly moving continental plate carrying India bumped against Asia. The rocks on the sea floor between them were squeezed together to form a high fold mountain range, the Himalayas.

Most fold mountains have elaborate folds. Some folds are pushed over other ones. These may break away and be pushed over other rocks.

Mountain Blocks

Movements in the Earth crack the rocks near the edges of the plates, forming faults. The tugging and stretching movements of the plates make blocks of land move up and down along the faults.

When a block of land is pushed along a fault or between two faults, a block mountain is forced upwards. Sometimes, there is a rift valley alongside a block mountain. A rift valley forms when a block of land sinks down between two long faults.

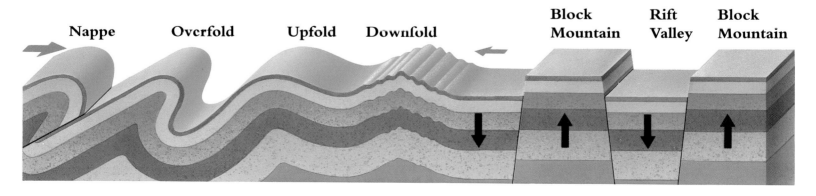

Nappe   Overfold   Upfold   Downfold   Block Mountain   Rift Valley   Block Mountain

The World's Mountains

The longest mountain chain in the world is the Andes, in South America, which stretches for 4,500 mi (7,200 km). The next longest is the Rockies in North America.

The Alps, the Himalayas, and the Andes are young fold mountains and are still rising. The Great Dividing Range in Australia is an ancient fold mountain range that has been worn down and then lifted up as a block mountain range.

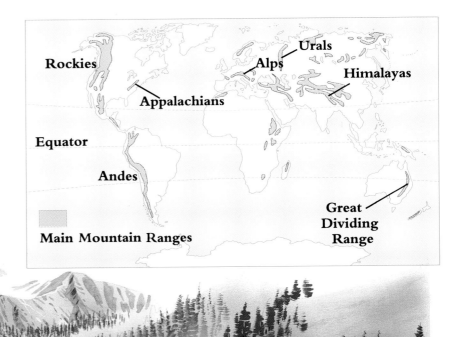

Rockies
Urals
Alps
Himalayas
Appalachians
Equator
Andes
Great Dividing Range

Main Mountain Ranges

Glacier

Scree

Worn Away

Mountain ranges are growing very slowly but they are also being worn away at the same time. Frost and ice in cracks shatter and break up the rocks. Stones and boulders, loosened by rain, may slip down mountainsides and pile up in a long, loose heap, called scree.

Sometimes, huge amounts of rock are swept downhill in a few minutes by a landslide. An avalanche of snow, crashing down a slope, can carry away a whole mountainside.

Fast-flowing streams carry down gravel, small stones, and even boulders, wearing away slopes. Glaciers, rivers of ice, grind slowly downhill like a river, scraping out valleys. The wearing away of the land is called erosion.

The Appalachian Mountains in North America and the Ural Mountains in the Soviet Union are very old ranges. They were once higher mountains than they are today, but they have been worn down through millions of years of erosion.

Mountain Facts

The world's highest peak on land is Mount Everest in the Himalayas. It is 29,028 ft (8,848 m) tall. The world's highest mountain, from its base on the ocean floor, is Mauna Kea, on Hawaii. It is 33,474 ft (10,203 m) high but only 13,796 ft (4,205 m) is above sea level. The biggest rift valley runs through East Africa into southwest Asia and is 3,500 mi (5,600 km) long.

Under the Ground

Most of the Earth's land has now been surveyed and mapped but there are many caves under the ground that have still to be explored. And there may be more still to be discovered. The biggest cave systems of all are found in thick layers of a rock called limestone.

It is rainwater, seeping into the ground, that dissolves, or eats away, rocks such as rock salt. When rainwater contains carbon dioxide from the air and the soil, it acts as a weak acid on certain types of rock, such as limestone.

Water at Work
Water seeps through the soil and slowly eats away limestone.

It drains through cracks in the rock, widening them into pits and caves.

Over many years, the pits, passages, and caves become a large underground network.

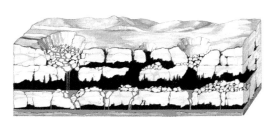

Underground Streams

Where limestone appears on the surface, the land is usually dry. This is because the rainwater seeps into the ground through cracks in the rock or through deep pits, called swallow holes.

The water joins underground streams that may flow long distances, through a complex system of tunnels and caves, before they come to the surface as springs. People, exploring the caves, float down the streams in inflatable boats.

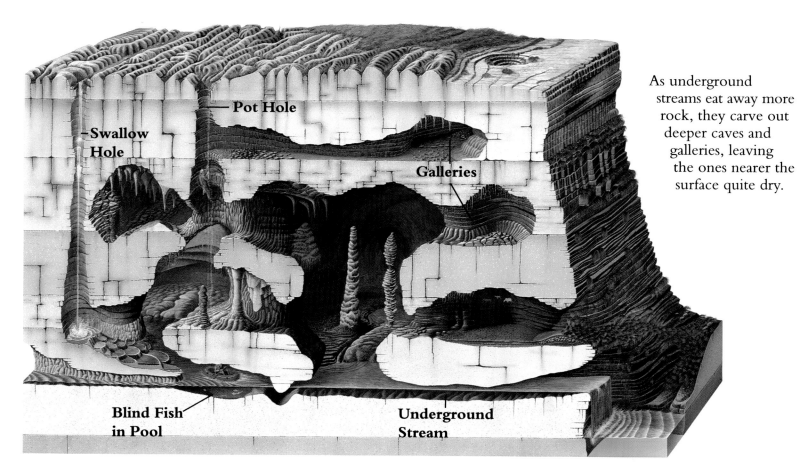

Pot Hole

Swallow Hole

Galleries

As underground streams eat away more rock, they carve out deeper caves and galleries, leaving the ones nearer the surface quite dry.

Blind Fish in Pool

Underground Stream

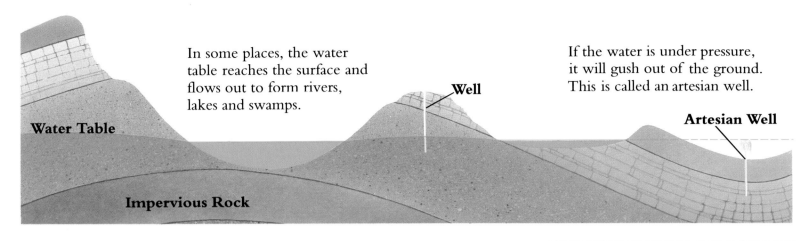

In some places, the water table reaches the surface and flows out to form rivers, lakes and swamps.

If the water is under pressure, it will gush out of the ground. This is called an artesian well.

Well

Artesian Well

Water Table

Impervious Rock

Water from the Ground

Rainwater seeps through other types of rock as well as limestone. Sandstone is a hard rock made up of grains of sand. Water can sink slowly down between the grains. It stops when it reaches an impervious rock layer – one that is so densely packed, the water can go no farther.

The top level of the water in rocks is called the water table. Wells can be drilled down to the water table and the water pumped up.

Growing Columns

Water seeping through limestone contains a mineral called calcite. Water dropping from cave ceilings leaves behind the calcite. Very slowly, a long finger, called a stalactite, grows downward.

Columns of calcite also grow up from water dropping onto the cave floor. These are called stalagmites. Some stalagmites and stalactites join up to form pillars. They are usually white but some are colored by traces of other minerals.

Underground Facts

Animals which live in caves use their senses of smell and touch to find their way around in the dark.

In the Mammoth Cave National Park in Kentucky, the cave system is about 350 mi (560 km) long.

The Sarawak Chamber in Malaysia is the world's biggest cavern. It is 2,300 ft (700 m) long and over 230 ft (70 m) high.

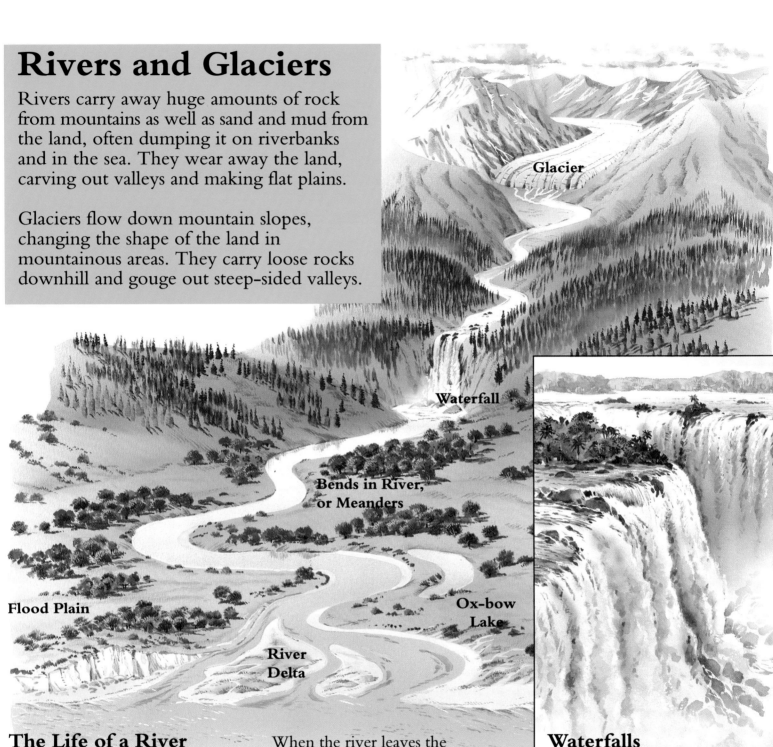

Rivers and Glaciers

Rivers carry away huge amounts of rock from mountains as well as sand and mud from the land, often dumping it on riverbanks and in the sea. They wear away the land, carving out valleys and making flat plains.

Glaciers flow down mountain slopes, changing the shape of the land in mountainous areas. They carry loose rocks downhill and gouge out steep-sided valleys.

Glacier

Waterfall

Bends in River, or Meanders

Flood Plain

Ox-bow Lake

River Delta

The Life of a River

Most rivers start in the mountains and flow down to the sea. At first, a river may be a stream formed by falling rain. It may begin as a spring on a hillside, or water from the melting end, or snout, of a glacier.

As it collects more water, the river rushes down the steep slopes. Rocks tumbling into it wear away the river bed. Slowly, the river carves out a deep, V-shaped valley.

When the river leaves the mountains, it flows more slowly. But it still wears away the land and becomes dark with mud and sand.

Before reaching the sea, a river may flow slowly across a flat plain. Here it wears away its bank on the outside of a bend. As the bends grow, the river may cut across them, leaving small lakes. Finally, the river dumps mud and sand at the river mouth.

Waterfalls

When a river plunges over a steep cliff edge or hard rocky ledge, it becomes a waterfall. The ledges form where a layer of hard rock is worn away very slowly by the water, while softer rocks below are worn away more quickly. The force of the falling water wears away the rock underneath the waterfall, forming a plunge pool.

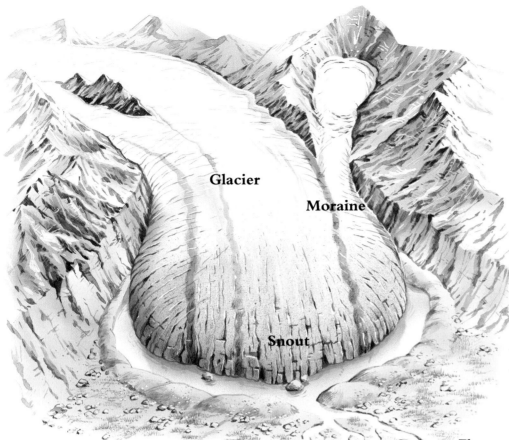

Glaciated Valley

**Streams Flow
from Melting Ice**

Glacier

Moraine

Snout

Rivers of Ice

Glaciers are rivers of ice. They form on mountains, where snow piles up in hollows. The snow gradually becomes pressed into ice. Finally, the ice spills out of the hollow to form a glacier.

Glaciers usually move by 3 feet or so per day. They carry rocks on their surface. Other rocks, frozen onto a glacier's sides and bottom, are its "teeth." As the glacier moves, it acts like a giant file, scraping away the land and carving out steep-sided valleys.

The loose rocks on and inside a glacier, called moraine, are dumped at the melting end, or snout. They may form a wall, enclosing a lake.

River and Glacier Facts

The world's longest river is the Nile in East Africa. It measures 4,145 mi (6,671 km) from its source to the point where it meets the sea.

About one fiftieth of the world's fresh water is frozen in the huge ice sheets in Antarctica and Greenland, in ice caps in such places as Canada, and in glaciers. There are glaciers in most of the world's high mountain ranges.

The world's highest waterfall is Angel Falls in Venezuela. It tumbles 3,212 ft (979 m) over a cliff in a highland area.

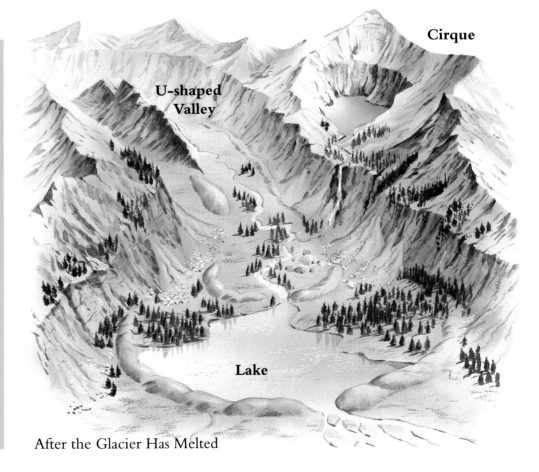

Cirque

U-shaped
Valley

Lake

After the Glacier Has Melted

Weather and Climate

In many places, the weather changes throughout the year and there are four main seasons – summer, autumn, winter, and spring. The seasons occur because the Earth is tilted on its axis. As it travels around the sun, first the northern half, or hemisphere, and then the southern half leans toward the sun and receives more of its heat and light.

On March 21, the sun is overhead at the Equator. It is autumn in the Southern Hemisphere and spring in the Northern Hemisphere. In the temperate regions, days and nights are the same length at this time of the year.

On June 22, the sun is overhead at the Tropic of Cancer. It is summer in the Northern Hemisphere and winter in the Southern Hemisphere. The North Pole, which is tilted toward the sun, has 24 hours of daylight, but the South Pole receives no sunlight at all, and has 24 hours of darkness.

On December 22, the sun is overhead at the Tropic of Capricorn. It is then summer in the Southern Hemisphere and winter in the Northern Hemisphere. The South Pole then has continuous daylight, while the North Pole is plunged into darkness.

On September 23, the sun is again overhead at the Equator. It is then spring in the Southern Hemisphere and autumn in the Northern Hemisphere. Again, the world's temperate regions have 12 hours of daylight and 12 hours of darkness.

The Atmosphere

The Earth is surrounded by a thick blanket of air, called the atmosphere. It contains the oxygen we need to breathe. It is also where all the weather happens. The air in the atmosphere may be warm or cool, dry or moist. This controls the type of weather we have. The air is constantly on the move, stirred up by the sun's heat. The way the atmosphere moves and changes causes the changes in the weather that some parts of the world have each day.

The atmosphere is made up of oxygen (nearly 21 percent), nitrogen (78 percent) and small amounts of other gases (1 percent). It also contains water vapor (the invisible gas form of water), and tiny droplets of water and ice that form clouds. From the clouds fall rain, snow, and hail. The Earth's gravity keeps the air from escaping into space.

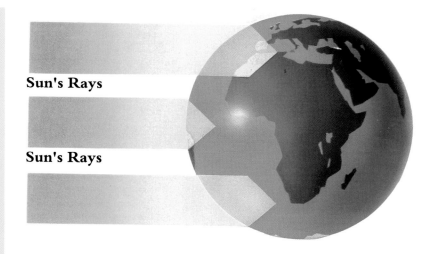

Sun's Rays

Sun's Rays

Hot Equator, Cold Poles

The hottest places on Earth are in the tropics, close to the Equator. The coldest places are around the North and South Poles. This is partly because the sun's rays have to pass through a thicker layer of air at the Poles than at the Equator. Air absorbs heat, so a large amount of heat never reaches the ground.

The Poles are also colder because the sun's rays spread over a much larger land area than they do near the Equator, so the polar lands receive much less heat.

Air Cycle

Near the Equator, the sun is very hot. It quickly warms up the ground which, in turn, heats the air above it. This warm air expands, or gets bigger, and rises. High up in the atmosphere, the air cools down again and spreads out to the north and south. It finally sinks down to Earth again at two zones called the horse latitudes.

Some of this air flows back across the Earth's surface toward the Equator. This causes the trade winds. Some air flows toward the Poles, creating the westerly winds. The westerlies meet cold, easterly winds flowing from the Poles. Winds do not blow directly from north to south. They are deflected, or swung sideways, by the Earth's rotation. This is called the Coriolis effect.

Warm air rises and cold air sinks.

Warm air from the Equator moves north and south.

Cold air circles around the Poles.

Atmosphere Facts

The air in the atmosphere presses down on the Earth and on our bodies. This is called air, or atmospheric, pressure. Above us is a column of air, weighing about a ton. We do not normally feel it because we have an equal pressure inside our bodies that balances it.

Air pressure grows less as you go higher up. At 18,000 ft (5,400 m) above sea level, the air is so thin that each breath you take has only about half the oxygen you get at sea level. This makes it difficult to breathe on high mountains.

The Water Cycle

The sun heats the water in the oceans which evaporates and turns into water vapor. This rises, cools, and turns into tiny drops of water, forming the clouds.

The clouds are blown over the land, bringing rain and snow. This falls into the oceans, or on land, where it flows downhill back to the oceans, completing the water cycle.

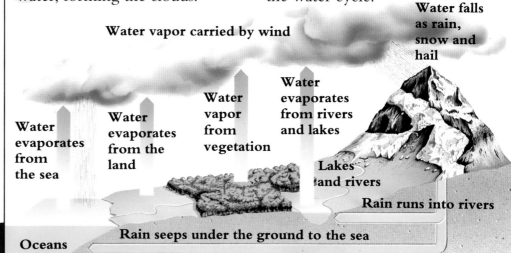

Water vapor carried by wind

Water falls as rain, snow and hail

Water evaporates from the sea

Water evaporates from the land

Water vapor from vegetation

Water evaporates from rivers and lakes

Lakes and rivers

Rain runs into rivers

Rain seeps under the ground to the sea

Oceans

Layers of Atmosphere

The atmosphere is divided into layers. The lowest layer, the troposphere, is where the weather happens. Above this is the stratosphere, a level that contains a gas called ozone, which blocks harmful ultraviolet rays from the sun. The next layer is the ionosphere, made up of the mesosphere and the thermosphere above it. The highest layer, the exosphere, merges into space.

Ozone Layer

A

B
50 mi (80 km)

31 mi (50 km)

C

5 to 11 mi (8 to 18 km)

D

A Exosphere
B Ionosphere
C Stratosphere
D Troposphere

Rain, Snow, and Hail

We are all affected by the weather, especially by the temperature, and by rain and snow. Information from weather forecasts helps us decide what clothes to wear when we go out and when to plan an outdoor activity.

Even on hot, cloudless days, there is moisture in the air in the form of invisible water vapor. The amount of water vapor in the air depends on the temperature. Warm air can hold more vapor than cold air. When the weather feels hot and "sticky," there is a lot of water vapor in the air.

There are three main kinds of rain.

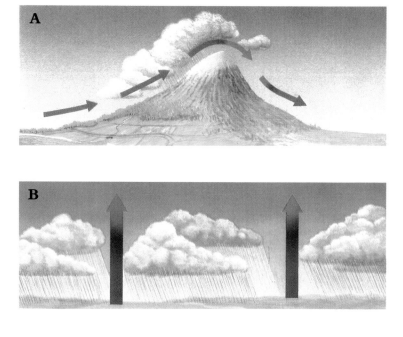

Before It Rains

When warm air rises, it cools and the water vapor it holds begins to condense into tiny drops of water. These join together to form clouds. Clouds can form when air rises and cools over mountains (**A**). Storm clouds form when moist air rises and cools rapidly on hot days (**B**). Clouds also form when warm air rises above cold air along a front (**C**).

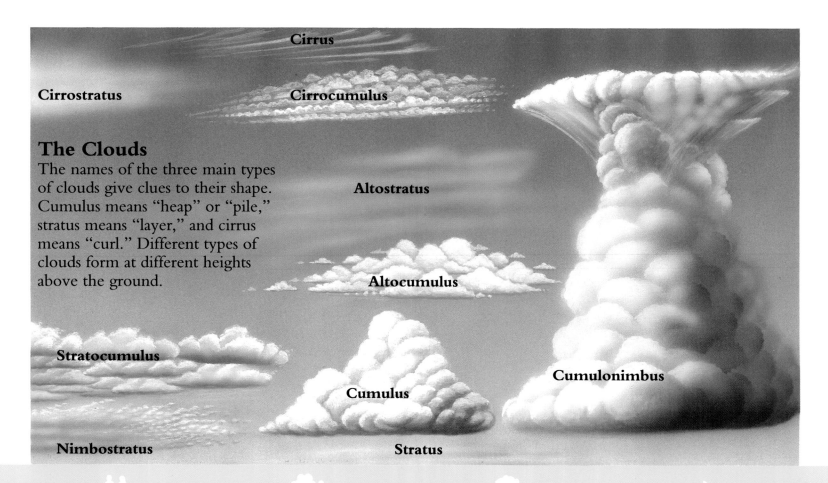

Cirrus

Cirrostratus

Cirrocumulus

The Clouds

The names of the three main types of clouds give clues to their shape. Cumulus means "heap" or "pile," stratus means "layer," and cirrus means "curl." Different types of clouds form at different heights above the ground.

Altostratus

Altocumulus

Stratocumulus

Cumulonimbus

Cumulus

Nimbostratus

Stratus

Rain

Snow

Hail

How Clouds Form

As the air cools, water vapor condenses around specks of dust to form tiny drops. Millions of drops form a cloud. The drops join together to form heavier raindrops.

Snow forms when water vapor condenses to form ice crystals in cold clouds. When masses of ice crystals collide and join together, they form a snowflake. Snowflakes always have six sides.

Sometimes, layers of water droplets freeze around an ice crystal to form a hailstone. They only form inside cumulonimbus, or thunder, clouds. Hailstones are usually about the size of peas.

The colors of a rainbow – red, orange, yellow, green, blue, indigo, and violet – are always in the same order.

What Makes a Rainbow

Rainbows form when the sun's rays are refracted, or bent, by raindrops or water spray. The water splits the sun's white light into seven main colors.

Sunlight

Raindrop

Rain and Snow Facts

In 1860–61, 1,041 in (2,646 cm) of rain fell in Cherrapunji, in India – the greatest rainfall in any one year. The greatest snowfall in a year was in 1971-72 in the state of Washington, with 1,222 in (2,850 cm).

Sometimes a second rainbow forms where the colors are in reverse order.

The Weather

The weather depends on the air around us, from day to day or from hour to hour. In some parts of the world, it is fairly easy to guess what the next day's weather will be like. It is always warm in places near the Equator, while it is always cold near the Poles. In many places in between, the weather may change very quickly. A day may start clear and sunny, cloud over in the afternoon, and clear again later.

These places are in areas where cold air from the Poles meets warm air coming from nearer the Equator. The boundary between the warm and cold air is called the polar front.

The study of the weather is called meteorology. Meteorologists are scientists who study information about the weather collected from all around the world. From this, they prepare forecasts.

Fronts and Depressions

When light, warm air meets heavy, cold air at a front, a basic pattern of air movement begins, called a depression. Where the cold air pushes underneath the warm air and forces it upward, a cold front is formed. As the warm air rises and cools, storm clouds may form, and it often rains heavily.

Where warm air pushes over the cold air ahead of it, a warm front occurs. As the warm air slowly overrides the cold air, several layers of clouds form.

A cross section of a depression showing a cold and warm front.

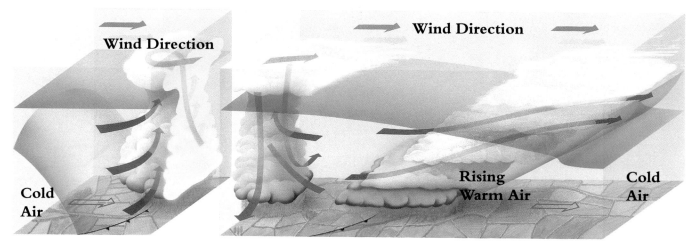

Wind Direction

Cold Air

Cold Front

Wind Direction

Rising Warm Air

Cold Air

Warm Front

Birth of a Hurricane

Hurricanes are huge, spinning masses of air. They form over warm oceans. At the center of a hurricane is a calm area, called the eye. Here, air is sinking, but around the eye, warm air is rising rapidly. Thick clouds form and strong winds blow at up to 185 mph (300 kph).

Hurricanes eventually die out when they reach land, but they can cause terrible flooding and damage to coasts. Tornadoes, although smaller, may be even more destructive.

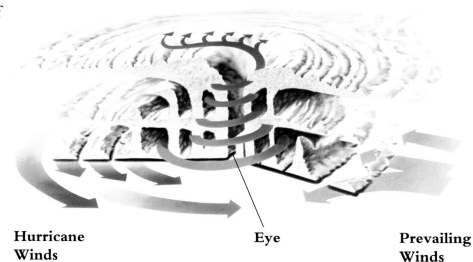

Hurricane Winds

Eye

Prevailing Winds

Thunder and Lightning

Thunderstorms are the most common storms. There are about 45,000 every day. They happen when warm air rises quickly in tropical areas or in depressions. Lightning occurs when electricity builds up in the storm clouds. It is released in huge flashes that travel between the clouds or between a cloud and the ground. The air along a flash of lightning is very hot. It expands very quickly and collides with the colder air around it.

It is this expanding air that makes the noise of thunder. We see the flash of lightning before we hear the thunder, because light travels faster through the air than sound.

Eyes in the Sky

Five geostationary satellites, like the one shown here, form a ring around the Equator, 22,500 mi (36,000 km) above the Earth's surface.

Weather Satellites

Meteorologists now use information from satellites to help them prepare much more accurate forecasts. The satellites orbit the Earth, sending back photographs of clouds and storms. Some satellites measure temperature and other conditions in the upper atmosphere. Forecasters can even follow the movements of a hurricane from satellite photographs and warn people who live in the hurricane's path.

Storm Facts

In mountain areas, where clouds form near the surface of the ground, flashes of lightning may be less than 300 ft (100 m) long. Over plains, where the clouds are higher, flashes may be 4 mi (6 km) long.

A hurricane, or tropical cyclone, hit the coast of Bangladesh in 1970, causing the deaths of about 300,000 people.

A tornado killed about 1,300 people in Bangladesh in 1989.

Waterspouts are like tornadoes but they form over the sea. The highest waterspout ever recorded, seen off the coast of Australia, was 5,015 ft (1,528 m) high.

Climates

The type of weather a place usually has over a long period of time is called its climate. Climate depends on several things. One of these is latitude, or how far north or south of the Equator a place is. Another is its closeness to the sea. Places near the sea often have milder climates than places far inland.

The world has five main bands of climates. Lands around the Equator have tropical, rainy climates. Deserts have dry climates. Places midway between the Poles and the Equator have temperate climates. Places near the Poles have damp, cold climates and the Poles themselves have very cold climates.

The World's Climates

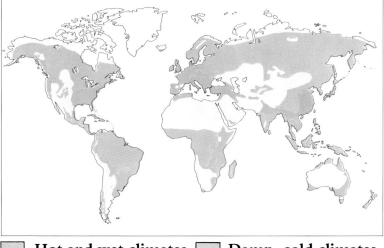

▨	Hot and wet climates	▨	Damp, cold climates
☐	Dry climates	☐	Very cold climates
▨	Warm, mild climates		

In the Forests

Huge forests grow in places with hot, rainy climates. They are called rain forests. The trees grow so close together that the forest floor is dark. Rain drips from the trees above and the still air is hot and damp.

34

The Rain Forests

The largest rain forests grow along the Amazon River in South America and in west-central Africa. Here, the trees are up to 165 ft (50 m) high. They are so tightly packed that little sunlight reaches the forest floor. There are also many climbing plants and tropical flowers, such as orchids.

Thousands of birds and many different mammals and reptiles, such as monkeys, sloths, and snakes, live in the trees. But vast areas of rain forest are now being cut down for farmland, mines, dams, and roads. Some scientists think that this might change the climates of places all over the world.

Tropical Grasslands

Bordering the rain forests are hot regions with a long, dry season. In these areas, forests grow only along rivers or in other places with water. The rest of the land is made up of tropical grassland, with a few scattered trees and bushes.

The largest area of grassland, or savanna, is in Africa. This is home to many animals, including lions, antelopes, buffalo, giraffes, leopards, and zebras. The numbers of these animals have dropped, partly because of hunting and partly because large areas of savanna have been turned into farmland. National parks have been set up to protect threatened animals.

Forest Facts

A few thousand years ago, rain forests covered about 14 percent of the Earth's land surface. Half of this has now been destroyed by people. The remaining forest contains at least 50 percent of all the world's plant and animal species. Yet the forests are still being cut down at an alarming rate to make way for farms, cattle ranches, and settlements.

Scientists have estimated that an area of rain forest the size of Austria is being cut down every year. At this rate, the forests will be destroyed by the year 2030.

The Dry Places

Deserts are the driest places in the world, with less than 10 in (25 cm) of rain per year. They cover about 14 percent of the land. In some deserts, there may be no rain for many years and then, during one great storm, large areas may be flooded.

Some deserts, such as the Sahara in Africa, are hot in the day but often cold at night. Other deserts, such as the Gobi in China and Mongolia, have bitterly cold winters.

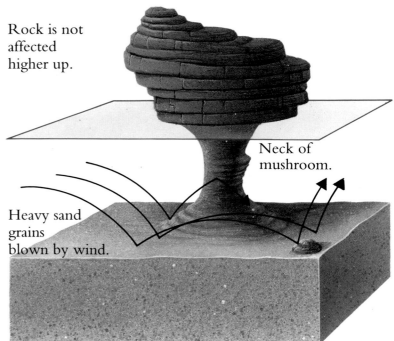

Rock is not affected higher up.

Neck of mushroom.

Heavy sand grains blown by wind.

Sand Dunes

Wind can blow the sand into crescent-shaped hills called "barchan" dunes.

These long ridges are called "seif" dunes. Their name comes from the Arabic word for "sword."

Wind and Sand

Sand covers about one fifth of the world's deserts. Sandy desert is often called "erg," another Arabic word. Large areas of desert are covered by loose stones. These are called "reg." There are also areas of bare rock, called "hammada." The rocks are worn bare by windblown sand, which acts like rough sandpaper.

The wind also blasts sand at large boulders. The sand grains bounce up against the rocks, wearing them away underneath until they look like giant mushrooms.

Arabian Camel

Banded Gecko

Life in the Desert

Desert animals are especially adapted for life in their dry homes. Snakes and lizards enjoy the heat, but even they shelter underground during the hottest parts of the day and the cold nights. Some lizards have transparent eyelids to protect their eyes from sand. Many animals store precious water in their bodies. Camels can go for many days without a drink.

Desert Jerboa

36

Desert Blooms

Plants that live in the desert have special ways of surviving long periods without rain. Cacti grow in the deserts of the southwestern United States. They have long roots that collect water from deep underground. The water is then stored in their thick, swollen stems.

Some plants bloom only after rain. Their seeds can survive for many years underground. After a storm, the plants spring to life and scatter their seeds within two weeks of sprouting. Then the desert is suddenly covered in a carpet of bright flowers.

Desert Water

Most desert people live in places called oases, where there is water. The Nile Valley in Africa is a huge oasis. People have farmed the land on the riverbanks for thousands of years. But most oases are water holes, where water from underground seeps up to the surface.

At other oases, people dig wells to tap the water lying far below the surface. A few family groups of wandering herders, called nomads, move around the desert in search of pasture for their camels, sheep, and goats. They travel from one oasis to the next to find water for themselves and their animals.

Desert Facts

The world's largest desert is the Sahara. It stretches across North Africa from the Atlantic Ocean to the Red Sea and covers an area of about 3 million sq mi (8 million sq km). The highest air temperature, 136°F (58°C), was recorded in Libya, in the Sahara.

Cave paintings from the central Sahara show that, about 10,000 years ago, the Sahara was much wetter than today. Grass covered most of the land. But the climate changed and, by 5,000 years ago, the region had become a desert.

Mild Climates

The tropics and the polar regions have very extreme climates and are very hot and very cold. Between them are large areas that have milder climates. These are called temperate climates. Most of the people in the world live in these areas. As a result, much of the original plant and animal life of these areas has disappeared.

Places with mild climates include the Mediterranean lands, which have hot summers and mild winters. They also include dry, temperate grasslands and regions that were once covered by great forests of deciduous, or leaf-shedding, trees.

City Wildlife

The spread of cities in the temperate lands has destroyed many areas where wild animals once lived. Some have adapted to city life. Foxes live in parks and gardens in Europe, raiding garbage cans for food.

In Canada and the United States, raccoons live in the chimneys and lofts of houses. Herds of wild dogs live around Kennedy Airport in New York City. Kestrels and pigeons nest on tops of tall buildings, while city reservoirs and ponds provide winter homes for waterfowl.

Trees and Tourists

The Mediterranean lands have hot, dry summers and mild, moist winters. These lands are around the Mediterranean Sea, but parts of the United States, Australia, Africa, and Chile also have "mediterranean" climates. Much of the land is farmed. Major crops include fruits, such as oranges, lemons, and grapes. The pleasant climate makes these places popular with tourists.

The Wheatlands

Temperate grasslands include the prairies of North America, the steppes of Europe, and the South American pampas. They have less rain than tropical grasslands, and winters are often cold and snowy.

They are used mainly to grow crops, or for grazing farm animals. The North American prairie is one of the world's greatest corn- and wheat-producing regions.

Bison Facts

Millions of bison used to roam across the prairies of North America. In 1850, about 20 million still grazed on the western prairies. In the late 1800s, the bison were killed by hunters for meat and because the land was wanted for farming.

By 1889, only 551 were left in the whole of the United States. Today, some animals are protected in national parks, such as the National Bison Range in Montana.

Deciduous Trees

Forests once covered huge areas of central and western Europe and eastern North America. Now, only small areas of woodland are left. Farmland, towns, and cities have largely replaced these great forests.

The trees in these woodlands are mainly deciduous, with a yearly cycle of activity which follows the changes in season. They shed their leaves in autumn, "sleep" for the winter, and bud again in spring. They are in full leaf for the summer.

Horse chestnut tree in winter, spring, summer, and autumn.

Cold Places

The land in Antarctica and Greenland is covered by two great ice sheets that never melt. Their cold, windswept polar climate is the harshest in the world.

Around the ice-covered areas of the Arctic lies a region called the tundra. Here, the ice and snow melt during the short summer. No trees grow in the tundra itself, but it merges with the evergreen forests of North America and Siberia in the USSR. These northern forests consist of coniferous trees, such as fir, larch, pine, and spruce, that can survive the bitterly cold winters.

The Poles

The North Pole lies in the Arctic Ocean, which is frozen over all year around. The Arctic is home to animals such as seals and polar bears.

The South Pole lies in the frozen continent of Antarctica. Few plants can survive on the ice- and snow-covered land, but the surrounding seas are very rich in plankton, tiny, drifting animals, and plants. This provides food for many fish, birds, and marine mammals.

Arctic Summer

During the short summer, the top layer of tundra soil melts. The soil below, called the permafrost, stays frozen. Mosses and lichens grow on the swampy surface. Caribou feed on the moss, and then move south to find food in winter.

Swarms of insects provide food for huge flocks of birds, which fly to warmer places in winter. Only a few hardy birds, such as snowy owls, winter in the Arctic.

Taiga Trees

Coniferous trees in the taiga forests are specially adapted to the cold weather. Their narrow, conical shapes prevent snow from piling up on and snapping their branches.

Many trees have thick bark to keep them warm. Birds arrive in the forests in summer to feed on the insects. Forest animals include bears, beavers, caribou, and wolves.

Cold Mountains

The higher up a mountain you climb, the colder it gets. The temperature falls by about 1°F for every 300 ft (6 to 7°C for every 1,000 m) you go up. As a result, even high mountains near the Equator have ice and snow on top. The temperature at the top of the Himalayas, the world's highest mountains, is as low as -4°F (-20°C).

Ice and snow

Tundra zone

Coniferous forest

Mixed forest

Deciduous forest

Grassland

Pole Facts

The lowest known air temperature, -128.6°F (-89.2°C), was recorded at the Soviet Vostok research station in Antarctica in 1983. In parts of Antarctica, the ice is 15,750 ft (4,800 m) thick.

In the Arctic, about 12,000 icebergs break away every year from the glaciers that flow down to the sea from the Greenland ice cap.

Climbing a mountain near the Equator is a little like a journey from the tropics to the Poles. This is because you pass through a whole series of climate zones on your way up. The zones range from tropical at the bottom, through temperate, then coniferous forests, and tundra, to polar conditions at the top.

The Planet and Its People

When people first started to farm the land, about 10,000 years ago, they began to change their world. They cut down forests and plowed up grasslands to make fields. Their animals ate the bushes and trees. Sometimes, this turned green landscapes into semi-deserts but, in some places, people watered deserts to make good farmland.

The first villages were built near the fields where people grew their food.

The farmers grew a mixture of crops and kept animals to feed their families. They sold anything that was left over. Today, many farms grow only one crop for sale.

Early farming methods did not pollute the rivers. The water in them was clean enough to drink and they were full of fish.

Today, more than two out of every five people live in towns and cities.

After the steam engine was invented, huge factories were built.

Smoke from factory chimneys can poison the air, killing plants and trees.

Sewage and factory waste drains into rivers. Many rivers near cities are now so dirty that fish cannot live in them.

People have cut down and burned more than half of the world's forests to clear land for farming.

Forests once covered nearly two thirds of the world's land surface.

Where People Live

People can live anywhere in the world where they can find food, water and shelter. Most people make their homes in places that have rain and are warm enough to grow crops for food. Where farmers can produce enough food for large numbers of people, huge cities have grown up.

A few groups of people have learned to make their homes in places where it is hard to grow food. Some live in dry deserts, some in the cold lands of ice and snow, and some in mountain areas, where there is little flat land for farming. Many live by hunting or by keeping herds of animals.

Desert Wanderers

A few people live in deserts. Some are nomads who wander the deserts in search of water and food for their animals. Others live at oases where a spring or well provides water.

Key to map
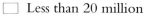
- Over 1 billion people
- 200 million–1 billion
- 100 million–200 million
- 20 million–100 million
- Less than 20 million

People Facts

The most crowded country in the world is tiny Macao, on the coast of China, with over 74,000 people per sq mi (28,000 people per sq km).

Apart from Antarctica, the least crowded country is Greenland. It has only one person for every 15 sq mi (40 sq km). Most of them live along the coasts, for much of Greenland is covered with ice.

Nobody lives in the great ice-covered continent of Antarctica, apart from a few scientists.

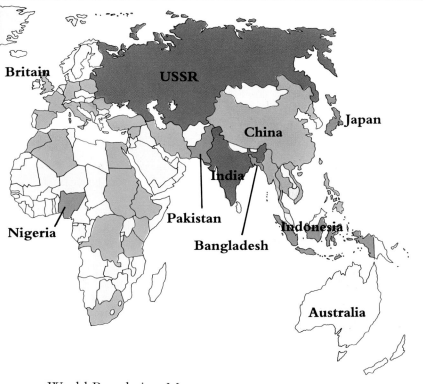

World Population Map

The Crowded Places

More than 5 billion people live in the world today, but they are not spread evenly across the countries. The world's largest countries are the Soviet Union and Canada, but fewer people live there than in warmer countries. China and India have the largest populations of any country.

Seven tenths of the world's people live in Europe and in southern and eastern Asia. In many other places, people cannot grow enough food to live. Much of Australia is hot, dry desert where nobody lives.

Ice Houses

In the frozen Arctic, the Eskimos, or Inuit, used snow to build winter shelters called igloos. They cut blocks of frozen snow to use as bricks. In summer, they lived in tents made of animal skins. Today, most Inuit live in modern towns.

Life in the Mountains

People cannot live easily on mountains. There is no flat land to farm and winters are very cold. Most people in mountain areas live in the valleys. Some farmers have summer homes on the high slopes. They move there in the spring to graze their flocks on the summer grass. Before the winter, they drive their animals back to the valleys.

Towns and Cities

Many towns began as markets where people from the countryside took the food they grew, their animals, and the things they made. There they traded them for the goods they needed. As more people settled in the towns, some towns grew into cities.

Other towns grew up where trade routes crossed, at safe natural harbors, or at places easy to defend against attack. In the cities, people developed laws and ideas of government. They built schools, universities, libraries, temples, and theaters.

At Home in Athens
The houses of ancient Athens were built of sun-dried bricks and had tiled roofs. Larger houses had two floors, with a kitchen and public rooms downstairs, and private rooms and bedrooms above. The family altar stood in a central courtyard.

Building on Trade
The meeting places for traders often turned slowly into cities. In France, several trade routes met at a ford across the Seine River. The village on an island in the river spread to the banks. Fishing and trade on the river enlarged the village, that later became the city of Paris, capital of France.

Reaching for the Sky
Many modern cities have huge skyscrapers. These very tall buildings were first put up in the 1880s. Growing cities needed more space to house more people.

Because of a shortage of land, people started to build upward instead of outward. The invention of electric elevators to replace stairs made this idea practical.

Upstairs, women weave clothes on looms.

Slaves cook the dinner in the kitchen.

A staircase leads upstairs from the courtyard.

Cities with over 5 million people

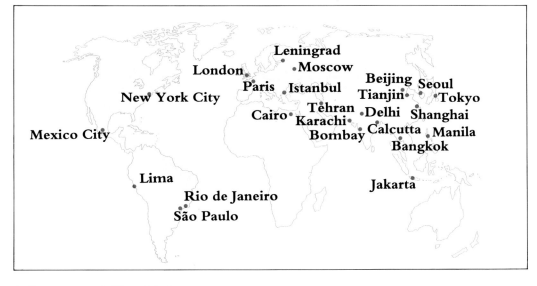

Leningrad
Moscow
London
Paris Istanbul
New York City
Beijing Seoul
Tianjin Tokyo
Tehran Delhi Shanghai
Cairo Karachi
Mexico City
Bombay Calcutta Manila
Bangkok
Lima
Jakarta
Rio de Janeiro
São Paulo

City Facts

Over 3,000 years ago, a people in India, called the Harappans, built cities, such as Mohenjo-Daro. They had wide streets, sewers, and impressive public buildings.

The world's largest city is Mexico City, where more than 18 million people live. By the year 2000, this will most likely have risen to over 24 million people.

About 90 percent of the people of Britain and Australia live in cities and towns. Only 5 percent of the people of Bhutan, in Asia, are town-dwellers.

The World's Cities

The world's largest cities began to grow more than a hundred years ago. Large numbers of people left the countryside and went to work in the factories in the cities.

With the new machines, worked by steam engines, people could make things quickly, instead of slowly by hand. The map shows where the world's largest cities are.

What People Eat

Early peoples lived by hunting animals and collecting plants, berries, nuts, roots, and eggs to eat. About 10,000 years ago, they began to grow crops and keep tame animals for food. The start of farming meant that there was more food for everyone.

Over hundreds of years, people found better ways of farming and grew more food. Today most food is produced on large farms. Only a few peoples, such as African pygmies and some South American Indians, still live by hunting and collecting wild plants.

Corn

Rice and Wheat

The most important food crops are cereals, such as wheat, rice, barley, oats, rye, and corn, or maize. Rice alone is the chief food of about half the world's people. Wheat was probably the first cereal to be cultivated and still provides the flour for most of our bread. Corn is now grown chiefly for cattle feed, but is also pressed for its oil.

Fruit and Vegetables

Most of the fruit and vegetables we eat have been specially bred over the years to be larger and juicier as well as easier to grow and harvest than the wild kinds. Small wild grapes have been developed to produce many different kinds of cultivated grapes, huge quantities of which are used to make wine. Many vegetables are produced in large quantities and then deep-frozen. This means that they are available all year-round.

Rice

Food Facts

India has more cattle than any other country. Most Indians believe that cows are sacred and will not eat them.

In the Middle Ages, chicken was eaten only by the rich in Europe. Today, it is probably the world's most widely eaten kind of meat.

In many countries, sheep, goats, buffalo, reindeer, and camels are kept for their milk. More than two thirds of the world's milk supply is made into butter, cheese, yogurt, and ice cream.

Bananas were one of the first fruits to be cultivated. There are now over a hundred varieties.

Food from the Sea

More than 20,000 different kinds of fish live in the seas, lakes, and rivers. Fish is a very good food and is particularly valuable to countries, such as Japan, that have little grazing land for animals.

Most of the fish we eat comes from the sea, caught in nets drawn by fishing boats. Some freshwater and sea fish are farmed in pools or floating pens. About one tenth of the world's supply now comes from fish farms.

At sea, fish are trapped in a round purse seine net.

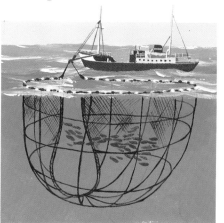

West Highland Bull

Tamworth Pig

Merino Sheep

Meat and Milk

Land which is too dry, too wet, or too steep to grow crops can often be used for grazing farm animals such as cattle, pigs, goats, and sheep. They provide meat and milk as well as wool and leather.

Farmers and scientists have improved farm animals over the years by careful breeding. Modern dairy cows give much more milk than their ancestors. Hens lay more eggs, and pigs put on weight more quickly.

There are many different breeds of animals to suit different weather conditions. Hardy, thick-coated animals, such as West Highland cattle and Scottish Blackface sheep, survive cold winters on bleak hillsides. Merino sheep, with their fine wool, are better suited to a warm climate.

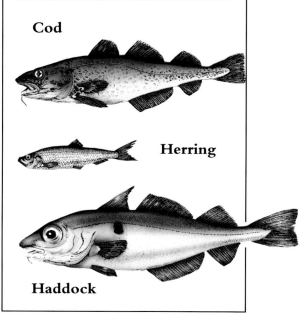

Cod

Herring

Haddock

The World's Farmers

In some countries, farming has not changed much for hundreds of years. Farmers have enough land to feed their families and they grow what they can. Their crops and animals depend on the weather, the soil, and the type of land they farm.

In the industrialized countries, farmers work huge farms with the help of modern machinery and science. Fertilizers and pesticides increase crops and control pests, and many animals are raised in sheds. Although few people are needed to work on the land, yields are high.

Watering the Desert

Some desert countries have fertile soils but no rainfall. In these countries, the deserts can be turned into farmland by irrigation, or artificial watering. One of the oldest methods is the waterwheel, which lifts water from wells, lakes, rivers, and reservoirs. The water runs though ditches to the crops.

Farming the Hills

In the densely populated areas of Southeast Asia, farmers build terraces along the steep hillsides to make use of the land. The terrace walls stop the soil being washed away by rain. Terracing makes flat, narrow fields for crops of rice.

Feeding the Family

In poor countries, farmers have only enough land to grow food for their own families. This is called subsistence farming.

The whole family works in the fields, although much of the work is done by the women. They have only hand tools to till the ground and harvest the crops. They must work hard to grow enough food, and may go hungry, or even starve, if their crops fail because of drought or pests. Many people in Africa and Asia live on these small farms.

Modern Machinery

Without machines, harvesting wheat is a long job for many people. They have to cut the wheat, tie it in bundles, cart it to be dried, and then thresh out the grain. Today, one person can do all this, driving a combine harvester. The machine cuts the wheat stems, separates the grain from the straw, cleans out weeds and chaff, and collects the grain in a big tank.

Combine Harvester

Farming Facts

People farm nearly one third of the world's land area. Two thirds of this is used to graze animals and the rest is used for crops. Over half the people of Africa and Asia live by farming, as opposed to only about 14 percent of Europeans and 4 percent of people in Canada and the United States.

About 800 years ago, an acre of wheat might feed two people for a year. Today, it can feed ten times as many.

The Earth's Resources

The Earth contains everything we need for life. The Earth's resources include vast areas of fertile farmland for growing food and other crops, and great forests for timber and fuel. There are huge deposits of useful metals and minerals for manufacturing, and different fuels that provide energy for factories and transport. But many of the world's natural resources are being used up very quickly and some can never be replaced.

The wood from forests has many uses. Many people burn it to cook their food and to keep themselves warm. Timber is used to build houses and to make furniture. Wood pulp is turned into paper and cardboard. Timber also has many uses in the chemical industry.

Vanishing Forests

When foresters cut down trees for timber, they plant saplings to replace them. But in the tropical regions, people are destroying the rain forests without replanting the trees. They are using the land to grow crops and graze animals. Millions of different types of plants and animals live in the forests. When the trees are cut down, there is nowhere for the animals and birds to live, and they begin to die out. Forests are also being damaged by air pollution, which stunts their growth and may even kill the trees.

Tree Feller

Processor

Logs of Standard Length

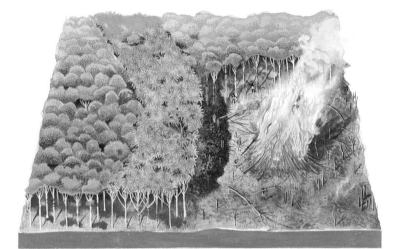

Part of the forest is cut down and burned.

The people build a village and grow crops on the land.

After a year or two, the people move on and the forest grows up again.

Natural Forests

Forests that are untouched by people have a natural balance of growth and decay, and may survive for thousands of years. As the old trees die, perhaps killed by lightning or by attacks by pests, they fall to the ground. Young trees grow up and take their places.

Cleared for Crops

The great forests of West Africa have long been cut down and burned to grow food on the cleared land. Because the soil is not very fertile, crops can be grown only for one or two years. The people then move on and clear a new patch of forest for farming.

Trees, bushes, and grass grow again in the cleared patches and the forest slowly recovers. After many years, the people can return. But now that large areas of forest have been destroyed, and the population is growing, the farmers have to return to old spaces before the natural vegetation has recovered.

Minerals, Metals, and Energy

The Earth is a great storehouse of metals and minerals. Some, such as diamonds and gold, are rare and precious. Others, such as bauxite, or aluminum ore, and iron ore, are fairly common. They are used to make many of the things we use every day.

In the Earth, there are also many valuable sources of energy. The main ones are coal, oil, and natural gas. They are called the fossil fuels. Another important source of energy is uranium. Uranium is used in nuclear power stations to make electricity.

Diamond

Mining the Ore

Metals are found in minerals, called ores. Miners remove rock and soil to reach ores near the Earth's surface. They then blast or scoop up the ore with machines. The ore is processed to extract the metal. This is called opencut mining.

Emerald

Rare and Valuable

Gold, silver, and platinum are called precious metals because they are very rare and valuable. Precious minerals include valuable gemstones, such as emeralds, diamonds, rubies, and sapphires.

Gold

The most valuable gems are very hard stones that will last for a long time. Some are also valued for their rich colors.

Fuel Facts

About two thirds of the world's electricity is made by burning coal, oil, and natural gas. These useful fuels will not last forever and will, one day, be used up, although there are still good supplies of coal. Scientists are looking for new ways of producing electricity.

One source of energy may be the heat deep inside the Earth. This is called geothermal energy, and is already used to heat homes and water in Iceland, New Zealand, and Japan.

Gold and silver have been made into jewelry for thousands of years. These precious metals are easy to hammer into shapes.

Silver

Oil and Gas Wells

Oil and natural gas were formed from the remains of prehistoric plants and animals many millions of years ago. Wells are drilled down to the rocks that contain them. Some of the wells are on land but many of them are in the seabed. Oil and gas are used for heating and to produce electricity. Oil is also used to make gasoline, chemicals, and plastic goods.

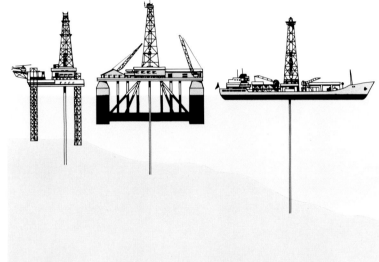

The first oil rigs, used to drill wells in shallow water, were built of wood. Later, rigs had many legs, sunk into the seabed. Legs of jack-up rigs extend to the bottom.

Floating rigs, used in deeper water, are anchored to the sea floor. In deep water, drills are lowered down to the seabed through holes in ships' hulls.

Useful Coal

Coal was formed from plants that grew millions of years ago. The plants died and were covered by layer after layer of mud. They were then pressed into a hard black or brown rock.

Coal is found on, and under, the Earth's surface. Today, miners use giant machines to cut the coal from the seams deep under the ground. China, the USSR, and the United States are the world's leading coal producers.

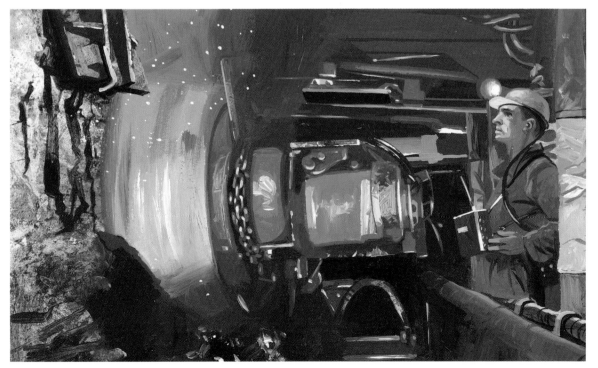

Using the Earth's Resources

The Industrial Revolution began in Britain in the late 1700s. It was a time of great change. Before the revolution, most people lived in the country and made goods by hand or with simple machines, often in their homes. During the revolution, factories were built, where the goods were made by the new machines.

These machines were driven by steam engines that burned huge amounts of coal to power them. Many other countries followed Britain's lead. They built bigger industries, produced more goods and became wealthy. Now, people in industrialized countries have higher standards of living than those who live by farming.

Burning coal produced thick, black smoke.

New Factory Towns

During the Industrial Revolution, thousands of people in Britain moved from the country to the new factory towns to work in the textile mills. Men, women, and even children labored for 72 hours a week in dangerous and unhealthy conditions. The steam-powered machines made cotton and woolen cloth that was exported all over the world.

Women worked in the mills making cloth.

Iron and Steel

The first countries to become industrialized were those that had plenty of coal and iron ore. Coal was burned to power the steam engines and machines used by industries. Coal was also used to fire the furnaces that produced iron from iron ore, for making the machines themselves.

Today, much of the world's iron is used to make steel. This is an alloy, or mixture of metals, and is very strong and long-lasting. It is used to make a great variety of goods, ranging from paper clips and saucepans to car bodies and oil tankers. In steel-making factories, the metal is heated in furnaces until it is a red-hot liquid. It is then poured into molds and cooled.

Railways and canals delivered the products.

The workers lived in rows of small houses.

Factory Facts

In industrialized countries, most goods are made by machine in factories. Only a few very expensive things, such as some clothes, are still made slowly, by hand.

The first factories were built near the coal and iron mines. Although coal is still used as a fuel, it is mostly burned in power stations to produce electricity. In modern factories, the machines are driven by electricity.

Computer Control

Computers are widely used in making goods today. They are used to control machines and work out answers to problems. Microprocessors are also very important. They are no bigger than a fingernail, but contain all the elements of a large computer.

Microprocessors are very small electronic devices. They use tiny silicon chips, on which there is an assembly of electronic components.

Factory Robots

Since the Industrial Revolution, many faster, more efficient ways of producing goods have been developed. Car-making began in the 1890s. Then, in 1913, in the United States, industrialist Henry Ford introduced the assembly line system into his factories. The car parts were carried along by a moving conveyor belt. Workers added parts to the car, or tightened screws and bolts, as it passed along.

This system speeded up the production of cars and made them much cheaper to build. In many modern factories today, robots controlled by computers have been developed to do much of the work on fast-moving assembly lines.

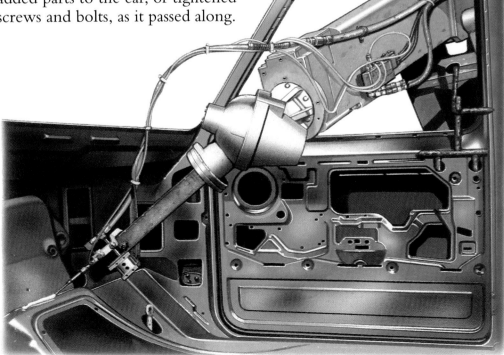

Damaging the Earth

People are damaging the Earth in different ways. As the number of people in the world increases, more of the countryside is being destroyed to make space for bigger cities and farms. One of the worst types of damage is caused by pollution.

The three main kinds of pollution are air pollution, water pollution, and land pollution. Factories and power stations pour dirty smoke and poisonous gases into the air. Water is polluted with chemicals, oil, and sewage. The soil is harmed by chemicals from fertilizers and pesticides used to produce bigger harvests.

Water Pollution

Water in ponds and lakes is polluted by acid rain and may kill the fish and wildlife in it. Pollution is also caused by farms and factories. Factories sometimes pump poisonous wastes, or may accidentally release them, into rivers or seas. Fish and other creatures die, but some survive and absorb the poisons into their bodies. When we eat them, we may also be poisoned.

Fertilizers and pesticides, the chemicals that farmers spread on their land and spray on their crops, are washed into the streams and rivers, polluting them. The fertilizers cause the water plants to grow very quickly, using up the oxygen in the water. The wildlife may then die.

In some places, untreated human sewage and garbage are pumped into rivers and the sea. Water used for bathing and washing clothes contains chemical detergents and soap that also pollute the water when it drains into rivers.

Main Causes of Air Pollution

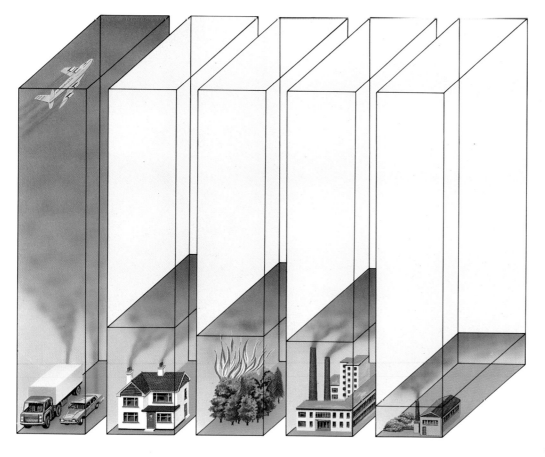

| Automobiles and trucks | Home heating | Burning forests | Factories | Burning waste |

Air Pollution

Air is polluted in many ways. In cities and industrial areas, the air contains gases and dust particles that make the atmosphere thick and dark. This air can be dangerous to all living things. It can damage food crops and buildings.

A main cause of air pollution is burning coal and oil. Gasoline and diesel fumes from cars and trucks cause foul air in cities. These fumes react in sunlight to produce a thick "smog." Other causes are heating houses, burning forests and waste, and factories.

Smoke and fumes from power stations and factories rise into the air. They mix with the rain, turning it into a weak acid. The rain is blown by the wind and often falls far away from the factories that caused it. It kills fish in lakes, kills trees, and eats away at buildings.

Polluting the Seas

Oil slicks can pollute huge areas of the oceans. They are usually caused when oil tankers run aground or collide and leak their cargo. One of the biggest oil slicks was caused by the bombing of oil wells along the coast of Kuwait in the Gulf War of 1991. The oil poured into the sea, killing birds, fish, and coral reefs.

Spoiling the Soil

The soil is a thin layer of loose material covering the Earth's surface. It is made up of worn pieces of rock and the remains of dead plants and animals. Soil stores the sun's heat and provides food and water for plants. When trees are felled or grasslands plowed up, rain may wash the soil away.

Farm machines press down the soil.

Roads use up land and may upset the natural drainage of rainwater.

In dry areas, winds may blow away fine soil and create a semidesert. This removal of the soil is called erosion. It can turn good farmland into a dusty waste.

Opencut mining can lead to soil erosion. Rainwater washes away the minerals from the mines, poisoning the land and the water.

The Earth's Future

Scientists fear that if people continue to destroy the natural world, the Earth may become unfit for us to live on. One cause for concern is the rate at which we are using up the Earth's resources, such as coal and oil. Unless we use them more carefully, or find alternative sources of energy, we will have no power for heating, lighting, transport, and industry in the future.

The study of how the Earth and all living things work together and depend on each other is called ecology. By looking at living things and the environment, and how we treat the Earth, scientists are trying to find ways to protect and save our planet.

Recycling the Waste

We throw away a huge number of things, creating enormous mountains of garbage. Many of these things could be used again to save the Earth's precious resources. Reusing materials is called recycling. Glass, metal cans, paper, plastics, and cardboard can all be recycled. Recycling not only saves on raw materials, but also uses up much less energy than getting the materials and making things from scratch.

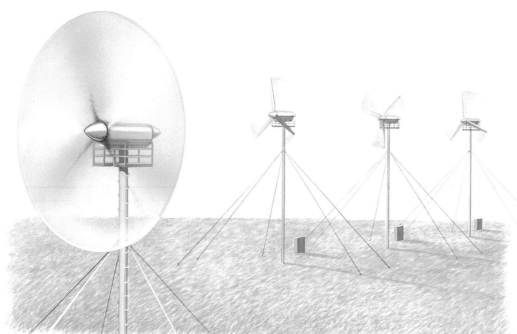

Alternative Energy

In many countries, scientists are looking for new ways of generating electricity. One method is to use the wind. Wind turbines, with huge, specially shaped blades, have been built in windy areas, such as on islands.

Wind farms are not the complete answer to fuel shortages. They need steady winds and large areas of open land, and are very noisy. They also cause unusual air currents and are a danger to birds. Over 1,000 turbines would be needed to replace one coal-fired power station.

Traffic Problems

Many people in industrialized countries already own a car. But cars are one of the main sources of pollution because of the huge amounts of poisonous gases they release into the air. Traffic jams bring city streets, as well as highways, to a standstill.

In some countries, cars are banned from certain city centers. Some governments have also banned the use of lead in gasoline, which gives off harmful gases. In many places, governments are trying to improve public transportation so that people can travel without having to use cars.

Wildlife Facts

To help save endangered wildlife, many countries have set aside special areas where plants and animals are strictly protected. Today, national parks and reserves cover about 4 percent of the world's land areas. This gives threatened plants and animals their only chance of survival.

In India, the tigers have been saved by being kept in reserves. Africa has the greatest number of national parks and reserves. The parks attract tourists and the tourist industry now provides many jobs for local people.

Saving the Whales

Overhunting has almost killed off several types of whales. Among them is the blue whale, the largest animal that has ever lived on Earth. In the 1980s, many countries with whaling industries agreed to stop killing whales, although some are still killed for what are claimed to be scientific reasons. If the ban lasts for some years, the whales should breed and increase their numbers.

61

Glossary

Acid rain Rain which has gases from factories and cars in it and is slightly acid. It wears away buildings and kills wildlife.

Atmosphere The layer of air around the Earth.

Avalanche A slide of snow, ice, and rocks down a mountain slope.

Axis The imaginary line joining the North Pole, the center of the Earth, and the South Pole.

Carbon dioxide A gas in the air. People and animals breathe in oxygen and breathe out carbon dioxide. Green plants take in carbon dioxide and give off oxygen.

Climate The average or usual weather in an area.

Coniferous trees Mostly evergreen, cone-bearing trees with needle-like leaves, such as firs and pines.

Continent A large land mass. The world's continents are Australia, Asia, Africa, North America, South America, Europe, and Antarctica.

Core The center of the Earth. The Earth's core consists of a solid, central core and a liquid, outer core.

Crust The thin, solid outer layer of the Earth, above the mantle.

Deciduous trees Trees that shed their leaves in winter.

Epicenter The point on the Earth's surface directly above the focus (point of origin) of an earthquake.

Equator An imaginary line around the Earth, halfway between the Poles.

Erosion The wearing away of the land, mostly by water and wind.

Evaporate To change from a liquid to a vapor.

Extinct An animal or plant species that has died out or been destroyed.

Fault A break, or fracture, in the Earth's crust along which the rocks have moved.

Fossil The traces of very old plant and animal life found in rocks.

Fossil fuels Coal, oil, and natural gas formed from remains of plants and animals millions of years ago.

Glacier A river of ice formed from compressed snow which moves slowly down a mountain.

Hemisphere Half of a sphere. The Equator divides the Earth into the Northern and Southern Hemispheres.

Hurricane A strong wind that forms over seas in tropical regions.

Lava Molten, or liquid, rock that flows from volcanoes.

Magma Molten (liquid) rock that forms deep inside the Earth.

Mantle The part of the Earth between the crust and the core.

Moraine Rocks, gravel, and debris carried by glaciers and ice sheets.

Orbit The path an object, such as the Earth, takes through space.

Oxygen A gas in the air which most living things need to survive.

Ozone A form of oxygen in a layer in the Earth's stratosphere.

Permafrost The layer of the soil in polar regions that is always frozen.

Plate A large piece of the Earth's solid outer layers.

Season A period of the year with a distinctive climate.

Solar system The Earth, the other planets, their moons, and other rocky debris that orbit the sun.

Temperate zones Zones between the hot tropics and the cold polar regions. Temperate zones have a mild climate.

Tornado A violent storm, or whirlwind.

Trench A long, deep trough in the ocean floor.

Tropics The hot region between the northern Tropic of Cancer and the southern Tropic of Capricorn.

Tsunami Fast-moving waves in the oceans caused by underwater earthquakes or volcanoes.

Water vapor Invisible, minute drops of moisture in the air.

Weathering The breaking up or decay of rocks by natural forces linked with the weather.

Index

acid rain, 58–59
air, 4, 28
  circulation, 28
  pressure, 29
Alps, 21
Amazon River, 35
ammonite, 6
amphibian, evolution of, 6
Andes, 21
Antarctic, 40, 41
Appalachians, 21
Arctic, 40, 41
asteroid belt, 9
atmosphere, 4, 6, 28, 29
  layers of, 29
atmospheric pressure, 29
autumn, 26
avalanche, 20, 21

bacteria, 6, 7
barchan dune, 36
bison, American, 39
bull, West Highland, 49

cacti, 37
calcite, 23
Cambrian period, 7
camel, 36
car, pollution, 61
  production, 57
carbon dioxide, 4
  in rainwater, 22
Carboniferous period, 6
carbon smear, 6
cattle, 49
cave, 22, 23
  animals of, 22, 23
  formation of, 22
cereal, 48
cirque, 25
city, 46, 47
  early, 46, 47
  large, 47
  modern, 47
  wildlife of, 38
climate, 34
  cold, 34, 40–41

climate, dry, 34, 36–37
  mediterranean, 38
  mild, 34, 38–39
  tropical, 34, 35
cloud, 28
  formation, 30, 31
  type, 30
coal, 55
cod, 49
computer, 57
coniferous tree, 40, 41
continent, 4
  moving, 10, 11, 14–15, 20
continental shelf, 12
  slope, 12
core, 11
  inner, 10, 11
  outer, 10, 11
Coriolis effect, 28
country,
  industrial, 56–57
  population, 44–45
  settlement, 44
Cretaceous period, 7
crust, 4, 6, 10
  plates of, 10–11
cumulonimbus, see
  thundercloud

deciduous tree, 38, 39
depression, 32
desert, 36–37
  animals of, 36
  people, 37, 44
  plants, 37
Devonian period, 6
dinosaur, 7

Earth, 4–13
  axis, 8, 26
  composition, 4
  damage of, 58
  formation of, 6, 7
  future, 60
  interior, 10–11
  orbit, 8, 9
  resources, 52–57

Earth, rotation, 8, 28
  surface, 14
earthquake, 11, 16–17
  epicenter, 17
  focus, 17
  zones, 16
electricity, 54–55
endangered wildlife, 61
energy, 54–55
  alternative, 60–61
  geothermal, 54
  nuclear, 59
  wind, 60
environment, 60
Equator, 8, 26, 28, 32
erosion, 14, 21, 24–25, 58
Eskimo, 45
Everest, 21
evolution, 6–7
exosphere, 29

factory, 43, 56–57
  assembly line, 57
  robot, 57
farming, 42
  crops, 48
  fish, 49
  fruit, 48
  grazing animals, 49
  machinery, 50–51
  modern, 50–51
  subsistence, 51
  terraced, 50
  vegetable, 48
fault, 11, 16, 20
fish, 49
  evolution of, 6
fissure eruption, 18
forest, 52, 53
  clearance, 53
fossil, 6, 7
  fuel, 54–55
front, 32
  cold, 32
  polar, 32
  warm, 32
fruit, 38, 48

galaxy, 8
gas, 6, 8, 55
gecko, banded, 36
geyser, 18
glacier, 21, 24–25
grassland, 35, 39
gravity, of Earth, 28
  of moon, 13
Great Dividing Range, 21
Gulf Stream, 13

haddock, 49
hail, 31
Hemisphere, 26
  Northern, 26
  Southern, 26
herring, 49
Himalayas, 20–21, 41
"hot spot," 18
hot spring, 18
hurricane, 32, 33
hydrogen, 9

igloo, 45
Industrial Revolution, 56–57
industry, 56–57
insect, evolution of, 6
  fossil of, 6
Inuit, see Eskimo
ionosphere, 29
iron, 56
irrigation, 50

jerboa, 36
Jupiter, 8, 9
Jurassic period, 7

lake, 23, 24, 25
  ox-bow, 24
landslide, 20, 21
latitude, 34
  horse, 28
lava, 18
lightning, 33
limestone, 22, 23

machine, 56–57

magma, 10, 18
maize, 48
mammal, evolution of, 7
mantle, 10–11
Marianas Trench, 13
Mars, 8, 9
Mercury, 8, 9
mesosphere, 29
metal, 54–56
    precious, 54
meteorology, 32, 33
microprocessor, 57
Milky Way Galaxy, 8
mineral, 54–56
mining, 54, 55
    coal, 55
    open-cut, 54
moon, 6, 9
    and tides, 13
    axis, 9
    orbit, 9
    rock, 9
moraine, 25
Mount St. Helens, 19
mountain, 11, 12, 24–25
    block, 20–21
    farming in, 45
    fold, 20–21
    temperature change, 41
    trees of, 41

Neptune, 8
Nile River, 25
nitrogen, 28
nomad, 37, 44

oases, 37
ocean, 4, 12–13
    current, 13
    ridge, 10, 12, 18
    trench, 12, 18
oil, 55
    rig, 55
    slick, 59
Ordovician period, 6
outer core, *see* core
oxygen, 4, 6, 28
ozone, 29

pampas, *see* grassland

Pangaea, 14
Paris, beginnings of, 46
people, 42–43
    farming, 48–51
    settlement, 44–47
permafrost, 40
Permian period, 6
pig, 49
    Tamworth, 49
planet, 6, 8
plankton, 40
plant, fossil of, 6
plates, 10–11
    and earthquakes, 11
    and volcanoes, 11
    movement, 10, 14, 20
Pluto, 8
polar front, 32
poles, 8, 28, 32, 40–41
pollution, air, 43, 58–59
    and cars, 60
    nuclear radiation, 59
    ocean, 59
    soil, 58–59
    water, 43, 58–59
population, 44–45, 47
pot hole, 22
prairie, 39
Precambrian period, 7

Quaternary period, 7

rain, 31
rainbow, 31
    colors of, 31
rain forest, 34–35
    animals of, 34
recycling, 60
reptile, evolution of, 6
    flying, 7
resources, 52–55
    forest, 52–53
    fuel, 52–55
    land, 52–53
    metals, 54
    minerals, 54, 55
rice, 48, 49
rift valley, 20, 21
river, 24, 25
    delta, 24

river, flood plain, 24
    life of, 24
    meander, 24
rock, 4
    erosion in desert, 36
    fossil, 6–7
    impervious, 23
Rocky Mountains, 21

Sahara Desert, 36, 37
San Andreas Fault, 16
sand, 36
    dunes, 36
sandstone, 23
satellite, weather, 33
Saturn, 8
savanna, 35
    animals of, 35
scree, 21
sea, 12
season, 26
seif dune, 36
settlement, 44–47
sheep, 49
    Merino, 49
shock wave, 17
Silurian period, 6
skyscraper, 46
snow, 31
solar system, 7, 8
space, 8
spring, 26
stalactite, 23
stalagmite, 23
star, 9
steam engine, 56
steel production, 56
steppe, *see* grassland
stratosphere, 29
summer, 26
sun, 6, 8, 9
    and seasons, 26–27
    and tides, 13
    rays, 28
swallow hole, 22

taiga, 41
    animals of, 41
temperate climate, *see*
    mild climate

Tertiary period, 7
thermosphere, 29
thunder, 33
    cloud, 30, 31, 32
    storms, 33
tide, 13
tornado, 32, 33
Triassic period, 7
trilobite, 7
Tropic of Cancer, 26
Tropic of Capricorn, 26
troposphere, 29
tsunami, 17
tundra, 40, 41

ultraviolet rays, 29
Ural Mountains, 21
Uranus, 8

valley, 24
    U-shaped, 25
    V-shaped, 24
Venus, 8, 9
volcano, 12, 18, 1(
    active, 18–19
    dormant, 18
    extinct, 18
    Hawaiian, 18,
    types of, 19

water, condensation, 30
    cycle, 29
    evaporation, 29
    table, 23
    vapor, 28, 30
waterfall, 24
waterspout, 33
waterwheel, 50
wave, 13, 17
weather, 26, 28, 30
    forecast, 32, 33
well, 23
    artesian, 23
    gas, 55
    oil, 55
wind, easterly, 28
    hurricane, 32
    trade, 28
    westerly, 28
winter, 26